ART GUIDE

- Simplified Art Course
- Mediums
- Visual Aids
- Art Projects

ART GUIDE

by Carvel Lee

Illustrations By The Author

Publishers

T. S. Denison & Company, Inc.

Minneapolis, Minnesota

Art Magic For You

Through A New Approach

To Art Fundamentals

Dear Art Enthusiast:

LEARNING in ART, is GROWING in ART—for teacher and pupil alike. Self-realization is the direct result of the acquisition of knowledge and skills. The ability to express thoughts and emotions in art can add zest to living and encourages personal growth.

Art can stimulate the imagination and can serve as an outlet for individual expression. This "Art Guide" book is designed to open the eye to beauty in countless everyday contacts and to alert the senses to the many moods and phases of art. This is a practical book—filled to bursting with art projects—providing the basic instructions and leaving the joy of creation to the reader.

As an art enthusiast, perhaps you enjoy experimenting or teaching art, but sometimes find it difficult to know where to begin. Then "Art Guide" was designed to meet your needs. In four steps are provided: a simplified art course and foundation, mediums to express art, visual aids that apply this knowledge to numerous subjects, and a section of tantalizing art projects.

As you glance through the following pages, may you discover ideas and inspiration that will make both your personal pursuit of art, as well as instruction in art, an exciting adventure.

The Author

Contents

Section One — Simplified Art Course

Section Two — Mediums

Section Three — Visual Aids

Section Four — Art Projects

Section One

Simplified Art Course

Drawing **is** easy — the secret is to advance step-by-step with a sound understanding and advance to more complex endeavors. These experiences can be the source of many hours of artistic fun.

A compact, easily-absorbed foundation of basic art principles — geared to the type of problems that are most apt to occur when you are exploring in art.

Contents

THE COLOR RAINBOW

A Color Experiment

You will need:

12 glass tumblers; red, blue and yellow food coloring; black and white tempera; water, a medicine dropper.

Red, yellow and blue are PRIMARY colors. By inter-mixing them we can obtain many colors. By adding black or white any shade, tint or tone is possible from these three basic colors.

1. Place three drops of red, yellow and blue food coloring in water in each of three tumblers. These are the primary colors.

2. Orange, violet and green are BINARY colors. They are made of TWO EQUAL parts of primary colors.

3. Red-orange, yellow-orange, red-violet, blue - violet, blue - green and yellow - green are TERTIARY colors. They are made of UNEQUAL amounts of two primary colors.

EQUAL parts of the three primary colors—brown.

A TINT: A shade **lighter** than a primary color. Add white.

A TONE: A shade **darker** than a primary color. Add black.

1 Primary Colors

Red   Yellow   Blue

2 Red {Yellow} Red {Blue} Blue {Yellow

Binary Colors

Orange   Violet   Green

3 Tertiary Colors

Red- Yellow- Red- Blue- Blue- Yellow-
Orange Orange Violet Violet Green Green

COLOR COMBINATIONS

WARM HUES

THE COLOR WHEEL

COOL HUES

▽ PRIMARY COLORS

○ BINARY COLORS

◇ TERTIARY COLORS

COLOR COMBINATIONS MEAN COLOR HARMONY

COMPLEMENTARY

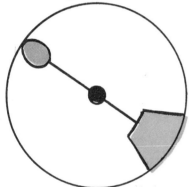

The color wheel shows the relation of colors to each other. The other five wheels show color combinations for harmony in application.

SPLIT-COMPLEMENTARY

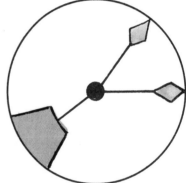

Colors opposite each other on the color wheel—use full strength or greyed.

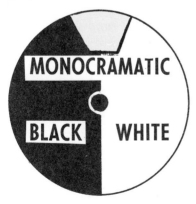

Divide **one** of the **contrast** colors for a more subtle combination of colors.

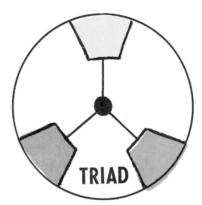

TRIAD

A color scheme employing varying self-toned, or light and dark values of just one color

This color scheme uses three colors at equi-distance points on the color wheel. Use any three colors in this related position for a close harmony.

ANALOGOUS

Any "three-in-a-row" colors on the wheel.

The Peacock Is A Proud Example Of COLOR Blending

You will need:

12 × 18" black and white construction paper, paste, water color paint, scissors.

Here is a way to experiment with color blending. Draw a peacock freehand on white paper. Cut out and mount on a piece of black construction paper. Using water paints in one color only, but using all its tints and tones, paint in the circular feather "eyes" as shown. Begin with the lightest tints and gradually darken the tones. You might try this monocramatic color scheme with all three primary colors.

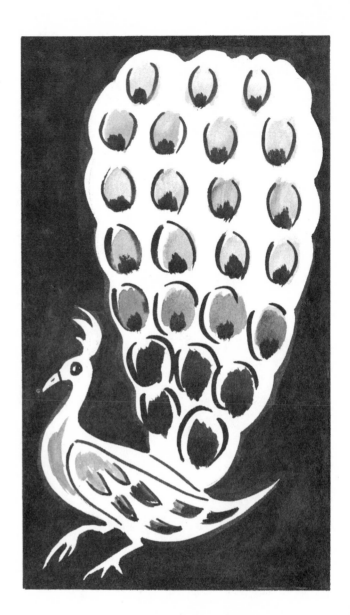

Color Combinations Are Something To Crow About

You will need:

Construction paper in assorted colors, paste, and scissors.

Draw a rooster on white paper. Divide his body into sections as illustrated. Cut and paste pieces of construction paper in these divisions to represent a complementary color combination. Use these colorful peacock and rooster designs to form a border.

Color Combinations
That Depict Seasons
A Cutting Project

Colors express feelings, moods, ideas and thoughts. Red is exciting, full of vitality and warmth; blue is cool, quieting and serene; green is relaxing yet is indicative of new growth and life; yellow is cheerful and buoyant. Combinations of colors suggest many moods in nature and in the seasons. Save scraps of bright papers and use them to create seasonal pictures.

SPRING — Using a complementary color scheme, cut out a violet umbrella and many yellow spring blossoms. Mount on a grey-violet background. Add a pipe-cleaner umbrella handle.

SUMMER — A triad color scheme is well suited to depict dragonflies. Cut oval wings and bodies from your choice of paper and paste to a white background. Punch tiny holes on each dragonfly's head and run thread through for realistic "feelers."

FALL — Fill a yellow-green wheelbarrow with blue-green grapes and bright red apples to illustrate a split-complementary color scheme. Use a brad to fasten on a wheel that really turns.

WINTER — Against a dark red fireplace (use construction paper with "brick" lines sketched with black crayon) paste "flames" cut from shades of bright-red and red-orange in an analogous color scheme. Cut white drinking straws in short lengths and paste in place to represent birch logs.

The FOUR SEASONS

Study the following scene — see how greatly the effect of the seasons vary the same subject. In the basic colors do you note overtones and tints of reflected colors? Note how the details are important to the overall effect. Draw and paint your version of the seasons.

The Cycle of Fruit
Reveals the Season

A Tearing Project

A basket and a ladder may be torn from paper that is folded. Tear tree foliage and trunk as indicated, you will need four of each. Mount on grey-blue background paper and add blossoms; birds; apples and picking equipment; and snow to depict the seasons as shown.

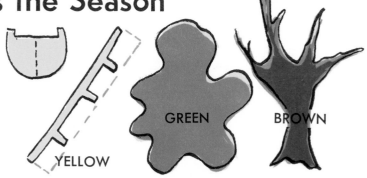

YELLOW   GREEN   BROWN

SPRING	SUMMER	FALL	WINTER

Flowers and Birthstones For Each Month Of The Year

Cut flowers of the months from colored crepe paper scraps. Paste on a harmonious background. Fringe flower edges where desirable. Add stem and leaf detail with crayons. Cut out a diamond-shaped opening below the flower. Paste a piece of colored cellophane behind the opening to represent the correct color for the corresponding birthstone of the month.

JANUARY

January — Carnation — Garnet
February — Violet — Amethyst
March — Jonquil — Bloodstone
April — Sweet Pea — Diamond
May — Lily-of-the-valley — Emerald
June — Rose — Pearl (Use white tissue)
July — Larkspur — Ruby
August — Gladiolus — Sardonyx
September — Aster — Sapphire
October — Calendula — Opal
November — Chrysanthemum — Topaz
December — Narcissus — Turquoise

MAY

Design

Experiment with Basic Shapes

Cut these basic shapes from many colors of paper. Combine in as many designs as possible.

Add irregular shapes also in many colors. Combine in various ways to obtain a variety of design and color effects.

Now using many shapes and colors of individual pieces discover the variety of design units that you can create. Try balanced designs as well as designs within a border. Try un-confined designs in a composition. Make your pieces touch, overlap or form a pattern.

A Repeat Design

Draw a single unit of design and then repeat to form a border motif.

Circular Design

Draw a circle with a compass, divide it in fourths. Make a design in one section and repeat in others. Make a repeat circle border design.

14

Rhythm in Design

Rhythm in a Border Design

Design can express many moods, movement or direction as well as rhythm, contrast and accent. Beauty of proportion, and tone contrast are important as well as how the design utilizes its space.

Rhythm in a Square

Rhythm of design is possible even within a confined shape if the movement is carried beyond the borders with a sense of continuation.

Rhythm in a Circle

A design within a circle can capture a feeling of motion that is good from any angle — a test of rhythm.

Realistic Subjects

Using a motif that depicts movement —paint a design in bright tempera colors.

An Abstract Motif

Draw a design with pencil and fill in the spaces with varying tones of crayon. Make the contrasts in color and shape bold in effect.

Composition

Cut various related objects from magazines. Arrange in a picture that overlaps the units in a pleasing composition.

A good composition is well-balanced both in form, light and shadow as well as tone contrast.

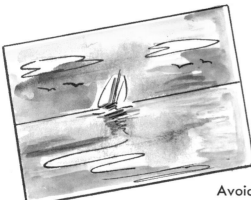

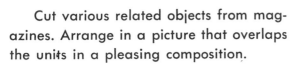

Composition

in Landscapes

Avoid monotony — find the center of interest and accent it. Often a PART is more pleasing than the WHOLE.

Paste-ups and Composition

You may wish to try a design several times before deciding on a final composition. For this purpose rubber cement is ideal. The pieces may be rearranged and lifted repeatedly without tearing.

SHIELD DESIGNS

An Experience in Design

The designing of shields is centuries old and the details may be very significant or denote a family crest. The possibilities in design and color arrangement are endless.

On tagboard lay out a number of shields and paint them with vibrant tempera colors. Design a shield that represents your personal interests.

Lovely Trivet Designs

A decorative accent for any wall would be striking trivet designs. By folding and cutting various ways many shapes may be obtained. Choose your favorites and trace around them on black poster board. Using a sharp stencil knife cut out the design. The trivets might be used as a wall decoration or as a gift box decoration for Mother's Day.

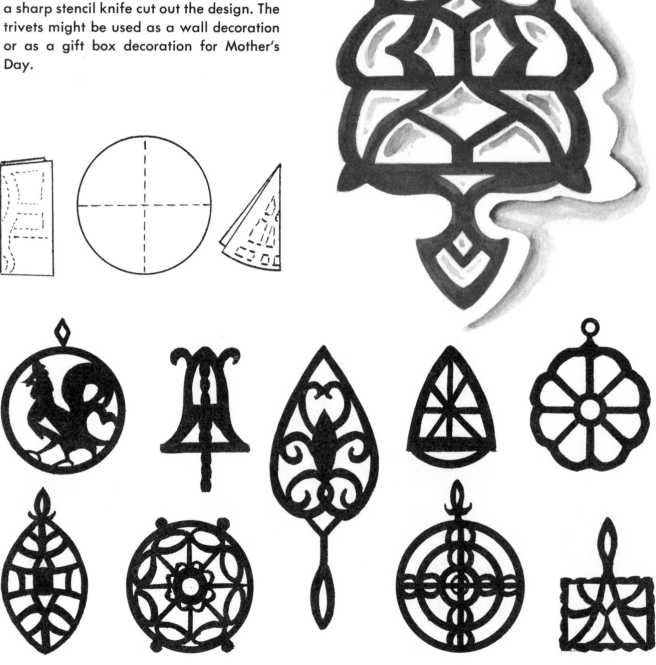

Layouts

The initial layout of any art project determines the success of the completed design. All the elements of balance, contrast and utilization of space are needed for any layout.

If you wish to enlarge or reduce a design mark the master off into sections. Mark your new paper off into the same number of sections. Copy the design, one section at a time, whether larger or smaller, from your original design.

Layout Sketches

Peasant Designs

Brush Strokes

Forming Designs

Peasant designs are usually executed in free-hand, flowing brush strokes, providing excellent practice in control and coordination. Flowers, leaves, fruit, birds, hearts are favored peasant motifs.

Flowers — Leaves

Border Motifs

Peasant Designs On Paper Plates

An inexpensive means of peasant design reproduction might be done on hard-finish paper plates. Using tempera paint in vivid hues originate a series of colorful plates. Protect the designs with a coat of clear shellac.

Uses For Design

Design finds expression in beauty as well as utility in many areas. Merchandise boxes, displays, paper items, newspaper and magazine illustrations, and greeting cards are typical of the uses for design layout.

Choose a specific objective and plan several designs that are suitable. Use good taste in the design balance and color areas.

Steps In Poster Design

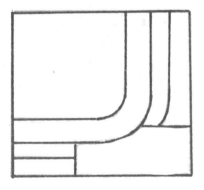  

Basic Lines **Focal Features** **Tone Contrast**

 # Design Uses

Design Jewelry

Although this jewelry is intended only for design purposes much can be learned in discrimination through this art project. Sketch design as shown on tagboard backings.

Rings

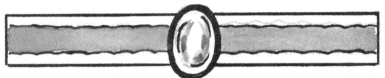

Cuff Links

Confetti Jewelry

Party confetti or paper punch circles in soft pastels may be used to design costume jewelry or Mother's Day cards.

 Paste Confetti On Dark Color Paper In Jewelry Effects

A Display Stand

To display your completed jewelry make a stand by folding a long strip of tagboard in even-spaced sections.

Bracelet

DRAWING IS EASY

Sketching

Sketch These Basic Lines and Curves

Combine Them In Various Shapes

Add Forms With Curves and Lines

Draw Simple Objects and Add Pencil Shading

Pencil Shading

Without shading a study will have a flat look. **With** shading contours have depth and dimension. Hold a pencil as shown —almost parallel to the paper, then shade with a sideways motion.

Heads, Faces, Expression

Find The Basic Shape   **Add Desired Detail**   **The Head Is Oval**

Practice With Ovals To Vary Head Position

Practice Facial Expression — Use A Coin For Circles

Profile   **Head Proportions**   **Front**

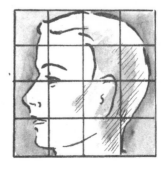

A side view of the head shows each part occupying an area in the square. The ear and nose are similar in size. The head is slender facing forward yet the features are in the same placement on the horizontal lines.

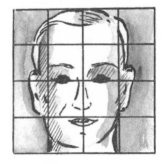

Hands and Feet

Inside of Hand

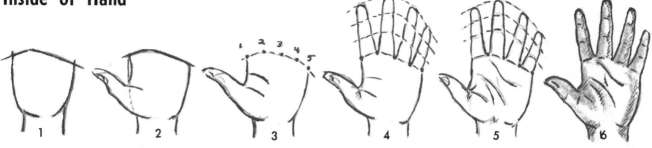

Hold up your left hand. Draw the "U" palm shape. Slant the top line like a roof. Add wrist lines and thumb. Place five dots as shown.

Add fingers, tapering the tips. Study your hand, adding joint and fold lines.

Outside of Hand

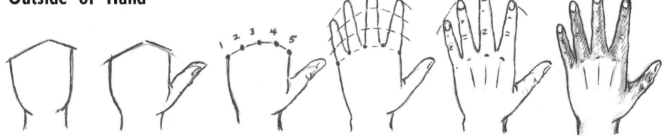

Look at the back of your hand, follow steps above to sketch. Add the thumb—noting that it is now **behind** the palm. Add joint and

knuckle folds and fingernail details. Add shading to both views of hands. Practice the hand and foot positions illustrated below.

Hands and Feet in Various Positions

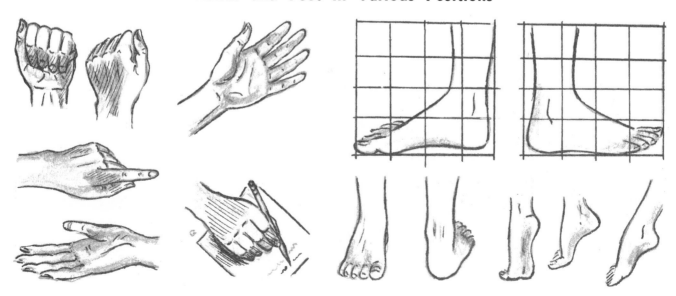

25

The Human Figure

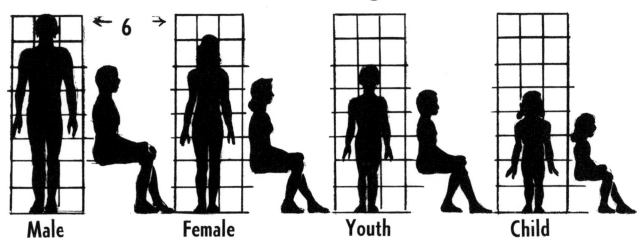

Male ← 6 →   **Female**   **Youth**   **Child**

Proportion

The ability to draw people is an asset. Approximate proportions for the average figure are shown. The head and trunk change least in growth—the legs lengthen most. Practice **line** figures that depict bone structure and **shape** figures that represent muscle and flesh.

Line Figures

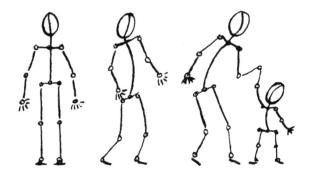

Shape Figures

Sketching Figures

Animals

Animal sketching is fun—note how body lines fall into shapes that overlap to give structure unity. Young animals have larger heads and rounded contours. For rhythmic, fluid sketches find the basic shape before details or shading are added.

Perspective

Eye Level

The dictionary defines perspective "As the science of representing depth on a flat surface, coordinated outlook, total comprehension." Study the cups shown above—note how the angle at which they are tipped is the level at which the eye views the cup.

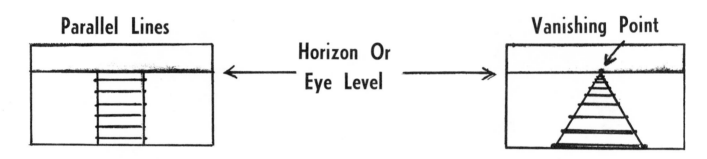

Parallel Lines

Horizon Or Eye Level

Vanishing Point

In drawing parallel lines, even though they are equal distance apart, they must be drawn as the eye views them. The point where the eye meets the **horizon** is called the **vanishing point**. The width of the tracks decreases to indicate distance.

A Highway In Perspective

vanishing point

Trees In Perspective

Eye Level

A Perspective Viewer

To visualize perspective, to help **see** the principle of **eye level** and **vanishing point**, make this viewer.

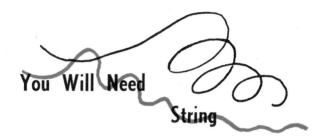

You Will Need String

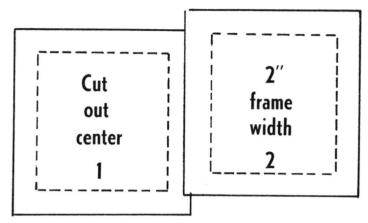

Cut out center 1

2" frame width 2

Two Pieces of Tagboard 8" x 8"

Step one—Begin with two pieces of tagboard and cut out the centers to form frames. Draw pencil lines 1" apart on the frame. Spread paste evenly over frame 1. Lay string on the paste as shown placing the red thread in the center.

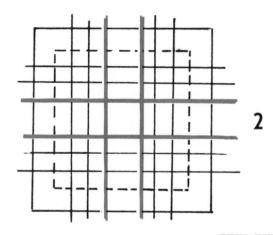

2

Step two—Trim the string even with the frame. Spread paste on the back of frame 1 and place on top of frame 2.

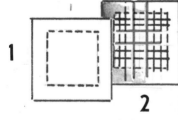

1

2

You now have a perspective viewer that will be helpful when sketching still life, outdoor scenes or room interiors.

Railroad tracks, telephone poles, fences—all recede to the vanishing point or eye level—framed by the red center strings. The lines of buildings will be revealed in clear-cut perspective when centered in the perspective viewer.

Imagination In Art

Stone Painting

The ability to see design or beauty possibilities in common objects is a challenge to the imagination. Look for stones that suggest an object. Paint with tempera and shellac to use as appealing paperweights.

Pastel String Designs

Several balls of string in pastel colors, construction paper, and paste are the ingredients of an imaginative art project. Dip the string in thinned paste and arrange on the paper in an original design.

Backgrounds For Hobbies

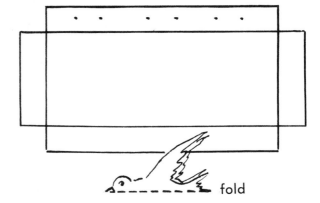

fold

For Hobbies You May Suspend

Airplanes with an airport scene, butterflies with flowers, rockets with a sky scene —any hobby that can be hung would be effectively displayed in appealing shadow box frames. A bird pattern is shown, cut from paper, gaily colored—they would be lovely hung in a wooded setting.

Window Backgrounds

Waxed Paper Window

Cellophane Window

Simple to make, striking in effect—window type backgrounds display insects, or pressed leaves or wildflowers to advantage. A triple-section piece of tagboard has a frame opening cut from the center panel. Two pieces of waxed paper or cellophane may have objects pressed between with a warm iron or pasted in position.

Nature Settings For Collections

Rocks, shells, figurines, or soap carvings could be displayed in these natural settings. Oval or square "stages" of styrofoam have tagboard "scenery" pinned behind them.

Rocks or Ore

Indian Handcraft

Shells

LETTERING

Square Block Lettering

3"

3"

Cut

A simple alphabet for many uses may be cut from 3" squares of paper in any color. Divide in one inch sections and fold as shown to form the individual letters. Larger letters may be made by enlarging the squares in proportion.

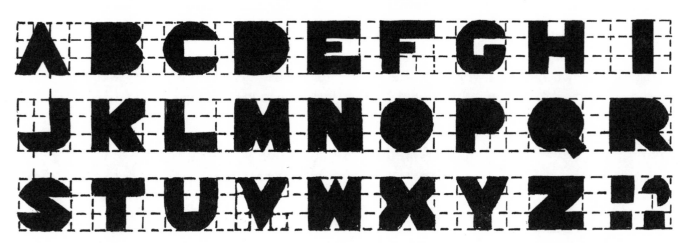

A B C D E F G H I
J K L M N O P Q R
S T U V W X Y Z !?

Rope Lettering

If you can write you can make rope lettering. On thin plywood, wallboard or styrofoam draw guide lines. In longhand write the message desired. With thumbtacks, tacks, or pins fasten the cord or rope over this outline.

Ric-Rac Lettering

Clever signs may be made with ric-rac. On poster board draw guide lines and sketch in lettering outlines. Paste ric-rac in gay colors in place as desired.

Choosing A Medium

SectionTwo
Mediums

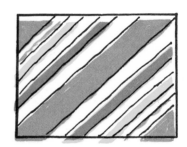

Contents

There is a great variety in the mediums in which art may be expressed . . . simple or elaborate they are an outlet for creativity.

Pen and Ink

Pen and ink is a striking medium with countless uses. Practice the varied tone effects shown and then combine them in your own original version.

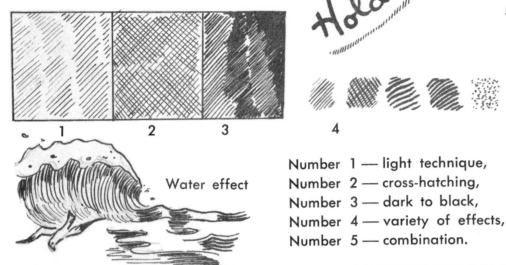

Hold Everything!

5

4

Water effect

Number 1 — light technique,
Number 2 — cross-hatching,
Number 3 — dark to black,
Number 4 — variety of effects,
Number 5 — combination.

Linoleum Block Printing

Effective for greeting cards, book covers, gift paper, bookmarks—block printing is a challenging medium.

1

2

3

4

5

6

1 — Draw design on the block. Be sure that the design is reversed sideways.

2 — Cut away linoleum—leaving only the part which is to print.

3 — Using the tip of the stencil knife, cut out the lettering.

4 — Slant edges away from the part that will print.

5 — Ink printers brayer and roll over the block. Press the paper on the block—smooth with the palm of the hand.

Spatter Designs

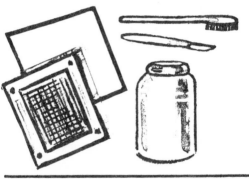

Spatter is an effective method for portrayal of designs. The soft blendings are lovely. Use a handmade screen-frame and a toothbrush or a spatter gun may be used. Thin tempera paint until it spatters readily.

Choose design motif and draw on stencil paper. Use a sharp stencil knife. Above is shown a complex spatter stencil. At the left is a simple motif. Hold the stencil to the paper to be spattered with rubber cement. When the paint is dry, remove the stencil and rub off the rubber cement.

Spatter technique lends itself well to Christmas cards, posters, gift paper, invitations and many other decorative uses.

Equipment Needed for Spatter

Stencil paper
Stencil knife
Screen and toothbrush
Spatter gun (optional)
Tempera Paint

Painting In Oil

Plan the sketch for an oil painting with attention to the masses rather than details. Canvas panels pre-mounted on boards serve well for beginning oil painters. Tube oils arranged in "color wheel" manner on a palette keep the various hues in a consistent pattern. Turpentine and linseed oil cups should be adjacent. Stiff-bristled brushes and a palette knife are also essential. Japan dryer will hasten the drying process.

Oil Painting Hints:

1 — Sketch in the painting subject lightly, keeping good composition principles in mind.
2 — Indicate the major light and dark areas, still avoiding too much detail.
3 — Paint in the intermediate hues. Add details.
4 — When the painting is thoroughly dry—apply a coat of clear varnish for protection.

Completed

Oil Painting

Water Colors

Water Color Hints:

Make a studied pencil sketch on good quality water color paper. Great luminosity and clarity are obtainable in water color paints. Use large brushes, change the water frequently. Use masking tape to fasten the paper to the drawing board.

1 — Draw scene, divide into areas.
2 — Use clear water, wet the sky and lake, using one-way strokes.
3 — Flow blue on the sky and the lake, fading the edge with clear water.
4 — Add red, blending into the blue. Let the paper show through in places.

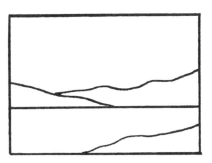 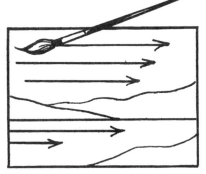 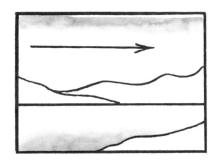

5 — Allow to dry, paint hills and ground areas in black and brown.

6 — Add trees, birds and rushes.

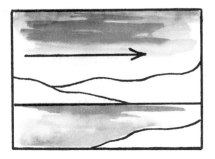  

Gouache Painting

Gouache is opaque water color that is quick-drying. It may also be called tempera, show card, poster or opaque water color. Gouache is easy to manipulate and lends itself to creativity. Illustration board is suitable for gouache. Sketch and paint a farm scene in gouache.

Clay

Clay is a very creative-potent medium. Originate your own objects for a highly satisfactory art experience. Oil clay is very pliable, for re-use but not lasting. Powder clay is mixed with water to putty consistency. Keep covered until used. When modeled, allow to dry, and paint with tempera or enamel paint. Moist clay may be modeled and will harden when dry. It may be painted or enameled.

Methods:

1 — Hand shaping, push and shape the clay.
2 — Joining, roll sections and press together.
3 — Coil, roll clay in coils, build to desired shape and smooth with fingers.
4 — Slab, roll clay on waxed paper with a rolling pin. Cut as desired and press sections together.
5 — Relief, roll a ball of clay and press to desired width. Carve the design and smooth with the fingers.

Turtles, Snakes and Snails

Use the coil method to create several species of snakes and snails. Use a combination of hand shaping and joining methods to make a turtle family. If moist clay has been used, you may paint these in realistic colors.

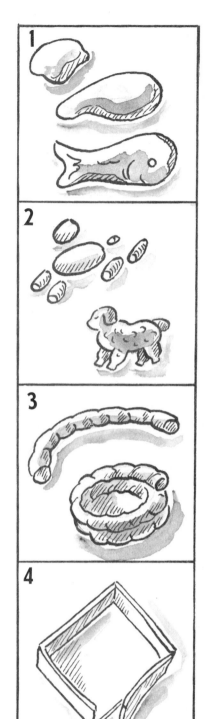

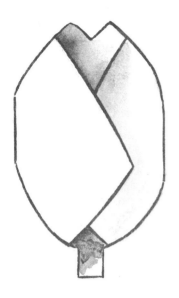

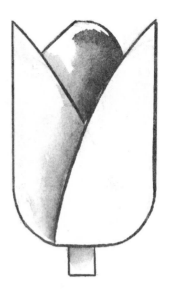

Paper Fun

Follow these general paper shapes to make folding tulips. Use as invitations or tape to pipe-cleaner stems for decorative use.

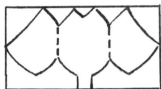

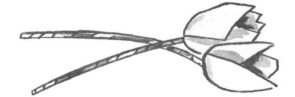

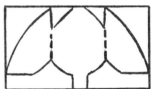

Easter Eggs

Cut Easter egg designs on the fold, mount against lavender, pink or green gift foil paper.

Paper Dancers

Design and cut dancers on the fold as shown. Use multiple folds for borders or cut and bend as shown for place card use.

Paper Tricks

Christmas Cut-Outs

Paper can be versatile in use. These cut-outs are suited to bulletin boards or Christmas cards. Fold a bright-colored paper down the center and cut out the Christmas tree. Lay this design on a dark-toned background. Cut a tree slightly smaller than the opening and staple them all in place. Add a tub and sticker stars.

Pet Parade

An appealing pet parade uses overlapping layers of crepe paper to provide fur, hair and feather effects. Combine with construction paper, add india ink details with a fine brush, and mount on harmonious backgrounds.

Cotton Capers

Snowman Door Design

One roll of inexpensive sheet cotton is cut to form a free-form snowman. Paste the snowman to a length of bright blue crepe paper. Add a black construction paper hat, broom, eyes and button, also a red scarf and a projecting nose. Cut silver paper doilies in small pieces and paste to the background as snowflakes.

Wooly Lambs

On a black background paste a white construction paper lamb's head and feet. Add pink hooves and ears. Paste cotton on lamb to form body. Add a blue ribbon bow.

String

String may be used for unusual effects. It is used here to denote an ice skater's spirals. An ice-blue paper background sets off a silhouette skater. Add string that has been dipped in thinned paste so that it will adhere where it falls. Paper clips make silver skates.

Wire

Stiff, fine wire will bend readily to form designs. Cut with wire snips. Fasten to a styrofoam background with wire staples. These may be used as trivots.

Yarn

Yarn combined with construction paper produces lovely fruit designs. Sketch and cut out the fruit, add crayon details, and use white glue to fasten colored yarns along the edges. Use black yarn for the basket and the border.

Rubber Bands

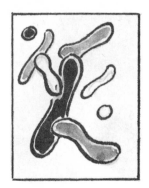

The robin, sketched with colored pencils, is struggling with a rubber band worm (run through punched holes and taped on the back). All sizes and colors of rubber bands are pasted in abstract design. Fill in the centers with colored inks applied with a brush.

Tempera Take-offs

Those familiar with tempera, either dry or moist, know its gay color possibilities. It can be used in unusual ways. In the snow scene deep-toned paper was used to accent white powdered tempera that was mixed with white glue and applied quite thickly. The tulips are done with moist tempera and paste mixed fairly thick. Both the above mediums were applied with a brush. The cut-out butterfly has dry tempera sprinkled over wet, crumpled paper.

Crayon, Chalk and Charcoal

Hazy Spring Bird Scenes

Crayon, chalk and charcoal — each are lovely when used singly — when combined they may achieve startling effects.

Use a bird book for reference and draw a bird and blossom scene. Lay crayon on sketch very heavily. Use the flat side of a pastel crayon and draw it across the scene. The chalk will produce a hazy, light and dark effect.

Brads, String and Crayon

On a box top, draw a simple design motif. Punch the box and place brads at accent points. Wrap string around the brads. Fill in portions of the design with crayon.

Halloween Ghosts

Rub pale yellow crayon over a light grey paper. Use the crayon tip to make a moon. Add black Halloween silhouettes and black crayon details. Rub charcoal over the entire scene for a eirie, ghostly effect.

Multiple Color Projects

Modern Sponge Effects

Cut a sponge in several pieces. Prepare finger paints in three colors in small containers. Sketch a three-part stencil design. Lay one stencil at a time on white drawing paper. Pat around the edges with a sponge dipped in one of the colors. Add two more stencil designs, each in another color. Allow design to dry between stenciling. Many modern effects are possible with this method.

Radiance Fringe Bells
On Oilcloth Place Mats

Novel bells would be unique done with this three-toned method. A stencil is laid on white oilcloth. With a stiff brush that has been dipped in fast-drying enamel paint, brush from the stencil outward to produce the radiance effect. Finish the edges with a pinking shears. These place mats may be wiped off for re-use.

Materials From Nature

Crushed Leaf Scenes

Nature is extravagant in providing art materials. Corn, pebbles, sand, seeds, acorns, weeds, nuts, shells, grains, grasses, bark — all may be used as art mediums. An unusual fall project utilizes leaves, dried and crushed, to make a scene. Twigs serve as graceful trees.

Cut a frame from black tagboard. Cut a piece of blue tagboard the same size. On this sketch a scene with hills leaving a blue sky and pond area. Collect fall leaves and sort by colors in bags. When leaves are very dry, crush in the bag. Cover one hill area at a time with paste. Sprinkle on the leaves and shake off the excess. Blend all colors of leaves and paste on as tree foliage. Add twigs for trees and glue in place. Add black frame.

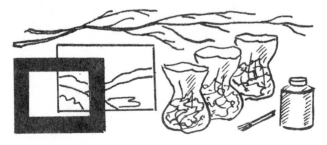

Pantry Art Materials

The kitchen and food shelves are a rich source of art supplies, that are inexpensive yet challenging. Rice, salt, coffee, cereals, baking cups, drinking straws, toothpicks, spaghetti, macaroni—the list is endless. A lively imagination can transform these materials into lovely art projects.

Popcorn Blossoms

Draw branches, leaves and blossoms with colored pencils. Flatten popped kernels of popcorn and glue to the branches for white apple blossoms.

Oatmeal Owl

This wise owl's secret origin is oatmeal. A yellow cornmeal moon glows against a pale farina sky. The owl's feet are rice kernels, his eyes are "doughnut" cereal, and his beak is a clove.

Coral Reef

Several persons might enjoy working together to create a sea scene. Use a variety-pack of cereals, rice, salt—to obtain unusual results. Rubber cement will hold fine-grained materials while white glue will hold larger cereal pieces.

Collage

A Study In Textures

A collage is an abstract composition made by utilizing the **textures** of various commonplace substances such as newspaper, buttons, beads, fabric, cork, felt, straws, broken jewelry, wallpaper, etc. Collect assorted materials and glue them to tagboard to create a collage.

Montage

A montage is the art of arranging in one composition **pictorial** elements borrowed from several sources so that the elements are both distinct yet blended into a whole. Gather photographs, newspaper and magazine illustrations, etc., that represent your interests. Make a montage by gluing them on bright shelf paper.

Visual Aids In Art

Contents

NIGHT AND DAY

Phases Of The Moon

Cut two circles of black tagboard and divide them into quarter sections. On the first circle draw the phases of the moon. On the second circle paste yellow paper over one quarter. Lay the first over the second and fasten with a brad. Turn to view the phases of the moon.

Sun Designs

Cut circles of graduating sizes. Design each circle in a sun radiance effect in many shades of yellow and orange. Cut them out. With the largest size at the bottom, place the auras one on top of the next. Place a brad through the center for a spectacular sun-glow effect.

The Village

At Night

Against a blue sky, place a black village silhouette. Paste on yellow windows for a night effect.

By Day

A yellow sky with a gray building silhouette are the ingredients of a day version. Add cars and people with crayon.

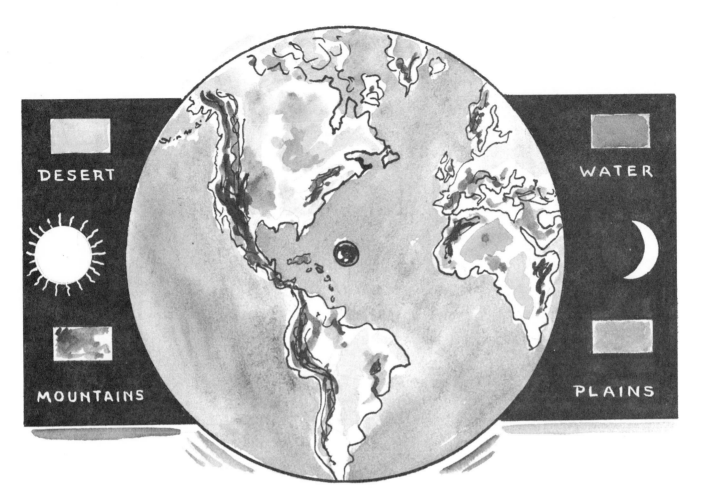

The Earth

A World Map With Realistic Effects

This art project could be enjoyed by a group. The earth is believed to rotate on its axis once every twenty-four hours. One third of the earth's surface is land. With the mediums described below, realistic relief, land and water areas may be denoted.

Cut a rectangular tagboard background and paint it with black tempera. Paste to this a sun and a moon in addition to the sand and salt samples as used on the map. Cut a large circle of tagboard and draw on it a portion of the world map. Indicate mountain ridges with the salt paste. Brush rubber cement on the plains, desert and water areas. Sprinkle the colored sands over the rubber cement and shake off the excess. Use a large brad to fasten the circle to the background.

Colored Salt Paste

Mix two parts salt, one part flour and tempera paint to a heavy paste. Mold as desired on the map.

Colored Sand

Fine white sand may be colored with bluing or crepe paper soaked in water to release the color.

Elements

The earth's materials are made of substances called elements. There are said to be ninety-two elements composed of solids, liquids or gases. Oxygen, carbon, hydrogen, uranium, mercury, silver and gold are typical elements. Centuries ago the Greeks believed that there were but four substances — fire, earth, air and water. Portray these ancient symbols in poster form. Stencils and spatter would be a suitable medium. Add colored pencil details.

Fire

Earth

Air

Water
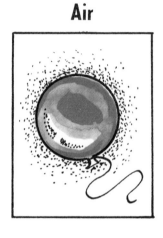

Weather

Weather Flash Cards

Tagboard cut in uniform sizes and the addition of torn scraps of construction paper would make interesting flash cards. Draw your version of weather flash cards, tear and paste on rain clouds, trees, snow, water, etc. The fog card might be in tones of gray with a yellow lighthouse beam.

Rain

Snow

Wind

Fog

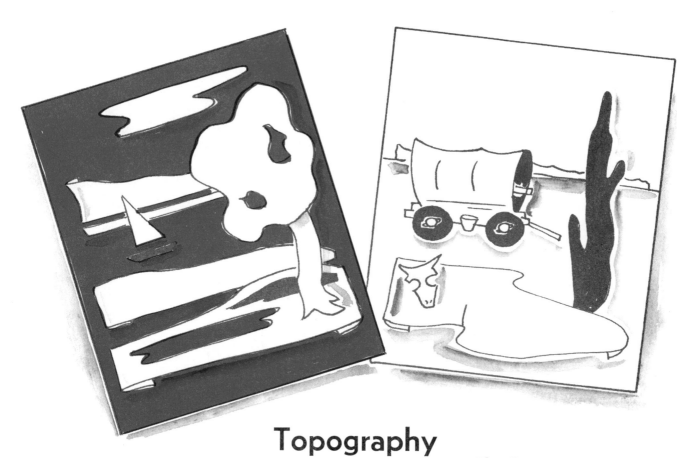

Topography

Lake Country

The physical features of our country might be portrayed in three dimensional posters. Construction paper would be a good medium. Some parts might be pasted on the background paper while others in the foreground

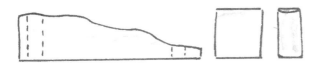

The Desert

might have "tabs" as shown. These tabs are to be folded under to make the pieces project. Paper pasted in small rolls on the back of the pieces also will help them project.

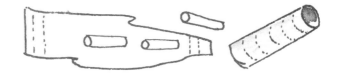

A Topography Mural

On a length of paper such as shelf paper or grocer's roll paper make your version of your local area. Use the three-dimensional method described above.

Trees

A Wet Chalk Art Project

Keep Our Forests Green

Colored chalk may be used as a "wet" medium by dipping in water. The tip or the broad side may be used. Immerse only the portion of chalk that will be used at once. White drawing paper would be a suitable background.

The first poster might portray a forest scene. Use three tones of green (flat side of chalk) for foliage. Using the chalk tip, add tree trunks in shades of brown. Add foreground detail and the wild creatures. Now you have portrayed the green forest—a valuable asset and the home of countless inhabitants.

The second poster indicates a burned-over forest with the wildlife fled or destroyed. Use tones of gray and the flat side of the crayon for the ground area and smoke. Red chalk indicates the fire that is still flickering. Black is used for the tree trunks.

Trees In Winter

Even the bare trunks of trees are lovely in winter. Make a background with the flat side of the chalk to indicate a soft evening sky and a shadowed snow foreground. With the chalk tip add graceful branches to show the beauty of barren trees.

54

Growing Things

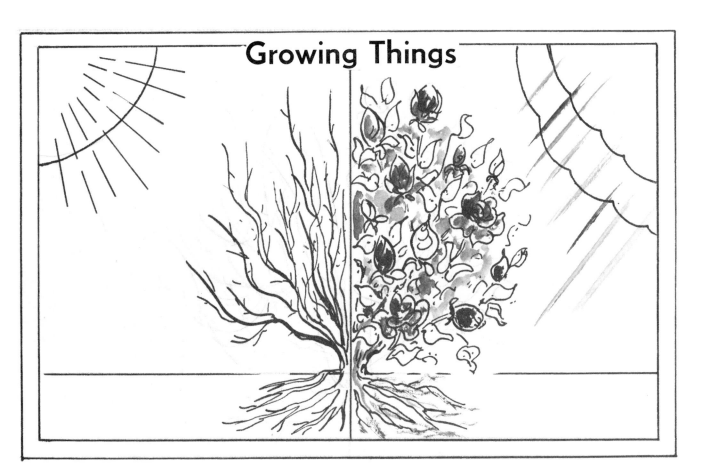

A Dormant Plant

This chart shows how moisture and the warmth of the sun arouses a dormant plant to burst into beauty. The background is a large rectangular piece of tagboard. Construction paper cut in shapes to indicate the sun, rain, clouds and the brown earth is then pasted in place. With tempera paints add the sun rays, rain streaks and the rose bush branches and roots. Show one half of the bush dormant—paint in roses and leaves on the other half.

Plant Needs

The chart below uses large paper chain links (pasted on the edges only) forming a mock-chain on a background. Print in your version of plant needs.

Paper Chain Link

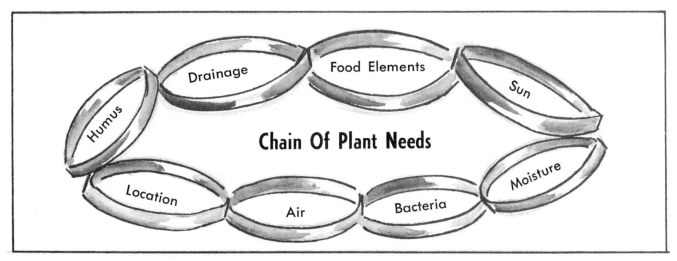

Humus · Drainage · Food Elements · Sun · Location · Air · Bacteria · Moisture

Chain Of Plant Needs

Seeds

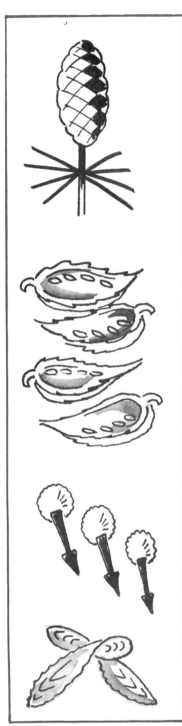

Seed Design Motifs

All around in the world of nature may be found the basis of design in seeds. Sketch many different motifs that you observe and arrange them in composition form. With textile paints use inexpensive cotton materials and utilize your seed designs for scarves, tablecloths and napkins.

Small Paper Plates
Display Seed Designs

Your seed designs would be lovely painted in tempera on small paper plates. Punch holes, insert bright ribbons to hang.

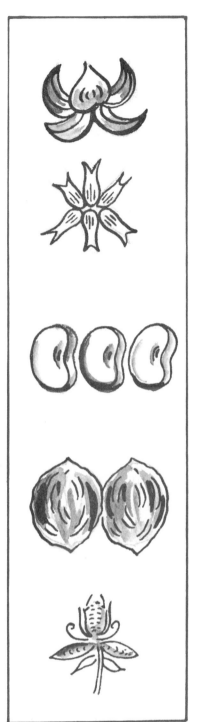

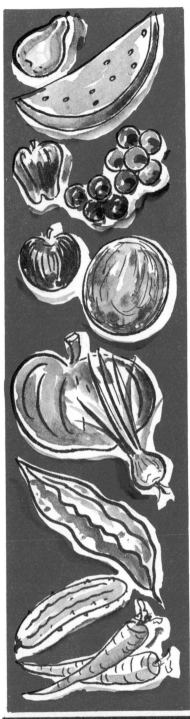

Fruits and Vegetables

In Water Colors
On Paper Towels

On white and pastel paper towels draw vegetables and fruits. The crinkled texture of the paper towels will add realism. Add details with water-color paints — flowing the paint on with generous amounts of water.

Arrange larger sizes of fruit and vegetable cutouts on black tagboard for a striking harvest frieze.

Party Place Cards

Create some fruit in tiny sizes, cut out and paste in a pleasing arrangement on folded white tagboard squares. Use for party place cards.

Harvest Bounty

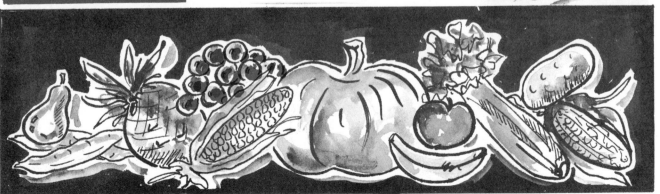

The Animal World

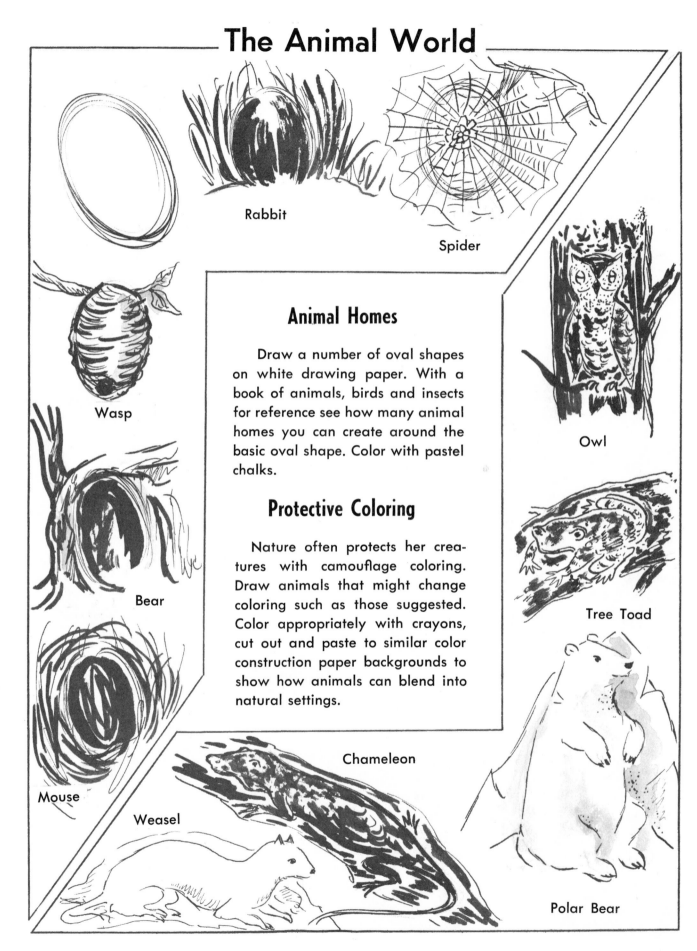

Rabbit

Spider

Animal Homes

Draw a number of oval shapes on white drawing paper. With a book of animals, birds and insects for reference see how many animal homes you can create around the basic oval shape. Color with pastel chalks.

Protective Coloring

Nature often protects her creatures with camouflage coloring. Draw animals that might change coloring such as those suggested. Color appropriately with crayons, cut out and paste to similar color construction paper backgrounds to show how animals can blend into natural settings.

Wasp

Bear

Mouse

Weasel

Owl

Tree Toad

Chameleon

Polar Bear

Swamp Life
Created From Macaroni and Spaghetti

The teeming life in the swamp may be captured humorously with macaroni and spaghetti. Use your imagination to interpret swamp life. Long spaghetti might be used for tall tree trunks. Short pieces, elbow, shell and ring types may be used to create turtles, frogs, alligators, cranes, snakes, fish and foliage. Use white glue to fasten to a pale green background. A pond might be added, cut from shiny blue foil gift paper.

Cornfields

On The Farm

Mailbox

Modern interpretations of farm life may be created by using bright-colored desk blotters, torn and pasted to construction paper posters. Keep the animals and objects modern and simple in line and design. Sketch in lightly on blotters and then cut out. Lay one color over another where desired.

Chicken Coop

The Barn

The Pasture

Farm Kitchen

The Chicken or the Egg?

Which came first—it's a debatable question—but the subject lends itself well to an amusing sequence poster. On shiny blue shelf paper paste white paper chickens and eggs. Add bits of bright paper for combs, beaks and eyes. Use toothpicks for legs and feet.

Sea Life

Beautiful Aquarium Window Panes

Use the panes of your window or make "aquarium" divisions with black tape. When the aquarium effect is completed you are ready to create the occupants. Sketch sea horses, crabs and several types of exotic fish in sizes that will fit your space. Cut these out and use as a pattern to lay on brilliantly colored transparent gift-wrapping cellophane. Attach the cellophane sea creatures to the window with rubber cement. Cut narrow, wavy strips of blue cellophane to indicate the water level. When the sun shines your window will sparkle with underwater beauty!

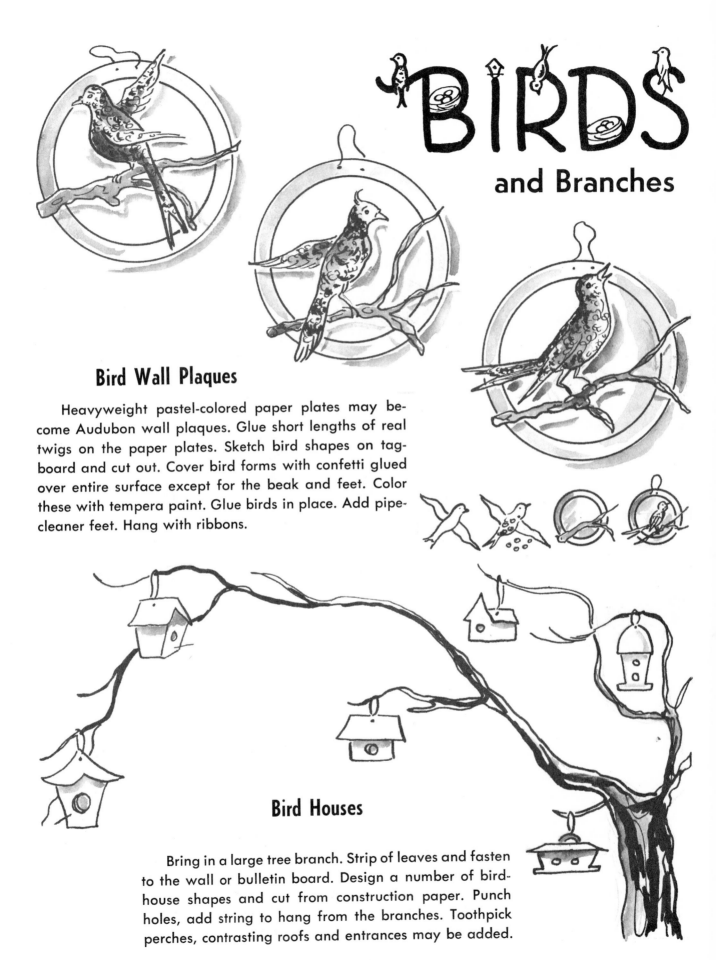

BIRDS

and Branches

Bird Wall Plaques

Heavyweight pastel-colored paper plates may become Audubon wall plaques. Glue short lengths of real twigs on the paper plates. Sketch bird shapes on tagboard and cut out. Cover bird forms with confetti glued over entire surface except for the beak and feet. Color these with tempera paint. Glue birds in place. Add pipecleaner feet. Hang with ribbons.

Bird Houses

Bring in a large tree branch. Strip of leaves and fasten to the wall or bulletin board. Design a number of birdhouse shapes and cut from construction paper. Punch holes, add string to hang from the branches. Toothpick perches, contrasting roofs and entrances may be added.

Butterflies and Moths

Cycle Of Cecropia Moth

Use white drawing paper as backgrounds for drawings of the interesting cycle of a moth's life. Paint your sketches with water color. Cut a cocoon and a moth on the fold as shown. Cut a slit in the cocoon so the moth may be inserted or removed.

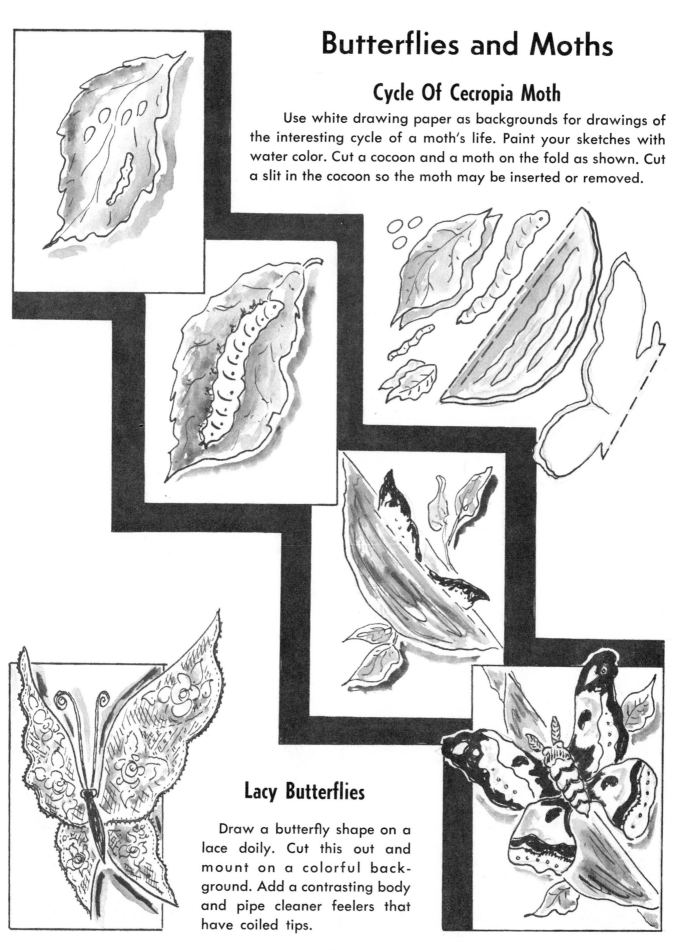

Lacy Butterflies

Draw a butterfly shape on a lace doily. Cut this out and mount on a colorful background. Add a contrasting body and pipe cleaner feelers that have coiled tips.

Insects

Caterpillars

Use a magnifying glass to study many types of insects. Cut a large leaf from green crepe paper and paste to a background. Punch holes in the leaf and insert yarn and ric-rac caterpillars.

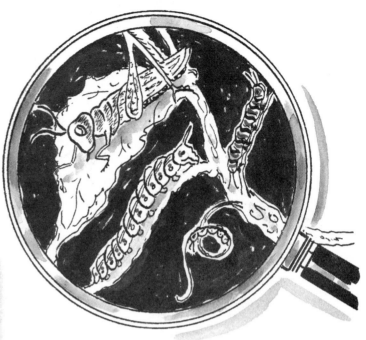

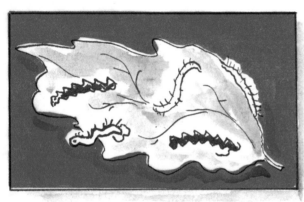

Fold a long strip of paper in equal sections. Cut a rounded worm head on one end. Punch holes and add pieces of string for feet and feelers. Use string to suspend the worms. Any slight breeze will cause the worms to wriggle.

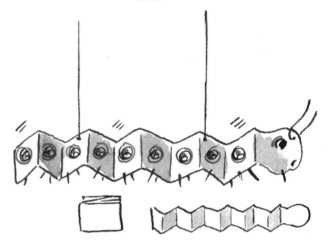

Insects—Above and Below Ground

Use your insect observations to create a mural. On blue shelf paper paste brown wrapping paper for an earth section. Paint insects, insect runways, plants and flying insects above and below the ground. Use tempera paint.

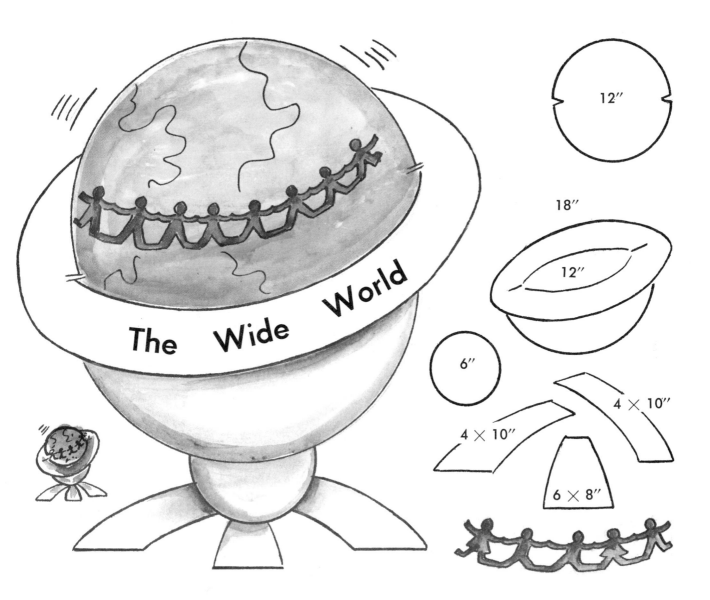

A Tilting World Globe

Draw and cut the individual parts of the globe and standard from tagboard. Draw and make slits where indicated. Color a portion of the world on both sides of the globe. Cut two chains of paper dolls (directions on page 39) and paste on both sides of the globe to represent the people of the world.

Building A Bridge Of Friendship Letters

Paste brown paper land sections on a blue background. Cut uniform-sized letters, add crayon detail, and paste in place as a bridge spanning the ocean. Add two paper people meeting in the center of the friendship bridge.

Progress
Searchlights Reveal The Progress Of A City Skyline

Use charcoal to make a smoky evening sky effect on blue tagboard. Use the broad side of the charcoal in short sideways strokes. Cut yellow searchlight beams and fasten to the background with a brad. Overlay (pasting only at bottom and sides) a city skyline cut from black construction paper. The searchlight beams may be pivoted realistically.

Transportation

Wheels Move The World

How important was the innovation of wheels in the history of transportation? The posters shown are only suggested. Originate your version of ancient or modern modes of transportation that employ wheels.

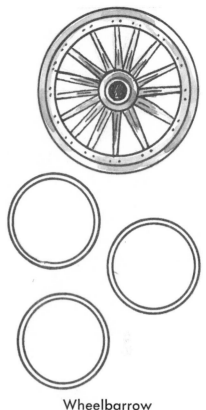

Fruit Jar Ring Posters

Fruit jar rings, using one or several, are the imaginative stimulant for posters. Look at a fruit jar ring—visualize how a poster could be built around it. Create several posters, pasting the wheels on a background and adding details cut from paper or colored with your favorite medium.

Jinrikisha

Covered Wagon

Wheelbarrow

Machinery

Design Motif

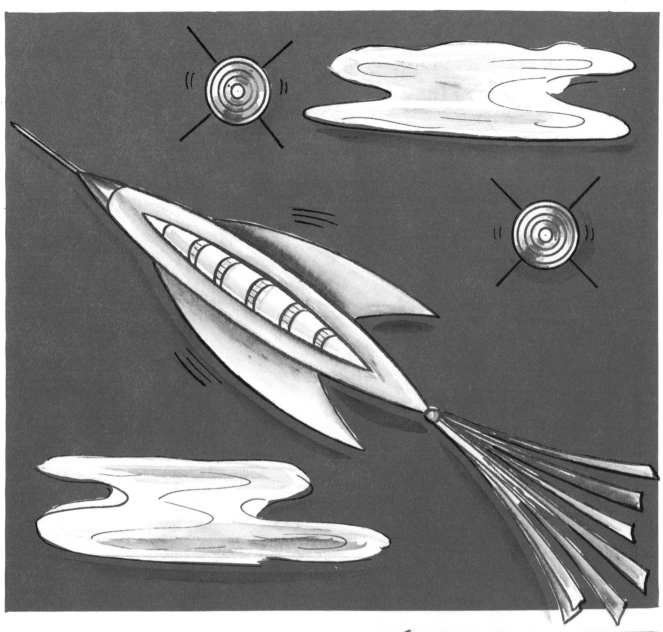

Space

Rockets and Satellites

The conquest of space—portrayed in this stunning bulletin board or poster idea. The background is deep blue heavyweight poster board. Pull two large pieces of cotton into cloud shapes and glue to the board.

A large fruit juice can provides the metal for the rockets and satellites. 1—Remove the can ends and glue toothpick antenna to them as shown. Glue to the board as satellites. 2—Use tin snips to cut the can open. Press flat and cut pieces 2 and 3. Add a red paper fuselage and nose cone to piece two. Glue the rocket to the board. Punch a hole at the rocket's base. Insert narrow streamers of red and yellow crepe paper. Tape them on the back to hold in place. Let's get into orbit!

The Sky

Have you been in the country at night—away from the city lights, and marveled at the brilliance of the low-hung stars? This art project helps visualize the constellations.

Deep blue tagboard forms the background. Cut a stencil that represents a country skyline. Place this stencil on the background, using fairly thick white tempera paint on a stiff brush, stroke upward. Remove stencil and allow the paint to dry. Above this soft skyline effect use white glue to fasten tiny sequin stars (available in hobby shops) to the night sky. The stars might form constellation patterns such as those suggested.

Youth Looks To Science As A Doorway To A Brighter Future

Science

This might be a group project for bulletin board use. Prepare a large piece of grey tagboard in a "smoke" shape. Cut a door opening in the smoke design as shown. Add an Alladin's lamp and the youth silhouettes. Make symbols that might represent the branches of science. Change the science symbol in the door daily to vary the poster.

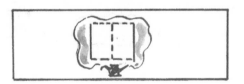

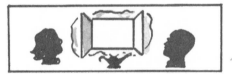

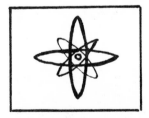

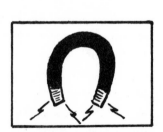

Community Pride

A Tearing Project

Clean up, paint up, fix up—a good slogan to keep a community and local area a pleasure to live in and travel through.

Where the litterbug is king—highways are unsightly and the area unattractive. When a community takes pride in its surroundings the whole vicinity is improved and appealing to view.

Make two identical placards using two sheets of light green tagboard. Tear white paper into a highway shape and paste in place. On the first placard add torn bits of paper, trash, old tires, billboards, a tumble-down house and a litterbug.

On the second placard place evergreens, trees, neat fences, a well-kept home—even a picnic or roadside area with a trash disposal. Compare the two scenes.

Our School

Floral Theme

Oilcloth-covered Standards

Beautify Lunchroom Tables

Where would be a better place to introduce beauty than in the lunchroom . . . and these appealing decorations may be wiped off with a damp cloth.

Make the standards as shown below. Cover them with gay oilcloth that may have the edges pinked with a shears. Add your own motifs to suit the season, holiday or occasion. Patterned or plain oilcloth may be used.

Holiday Motifs

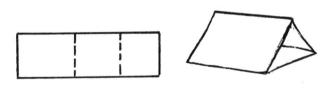

Fall — Apples and Leaves

Patterned Oilcloth

Art In The Home

Good Taste In Dinnerware

Discrimination has many facets. This art project is an experience in dinnerware design. Using a compass, draw circles on white, smooth-finished tagboard. Draw a cup shape. Cut out these plate circles and cup shapes.

Water colors would be an ideal medium to color your designs. Try a number of designs, choose your favorite, and analyze your choice. Make a display of the "china."

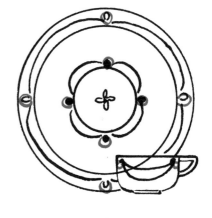

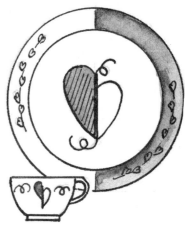

Arithmetic

Tone Number Designs

Use numbers in an interesting way by creating tone designs. Print each number in black India ink in the center of a piece of white drawing paper, or use a felt tip pen if you wish. Follow the number outline, keeping at an even distance from the number. Repeat this outlining until the sides of the paper are reached. Beginning with the first tone area, fill it in with a very light shade of tempera paint. Paint each successive area a darker tone.

Nail Design House Numbers

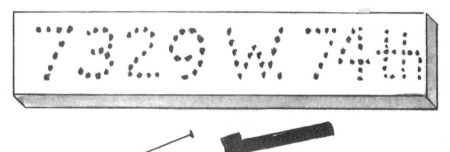

This project could be utilized as a gift for Dad. On a scrap piece of lumber, about 1″ × 3″ × 12″ in size, sketch the desired wording, either block or script lettering. Follow the pencil outline, pounding in nail holes. Rub the wood surface lightly and evenly with furniture wax. Rub Burnt Umber color oil paint over the entire board, being sure to fill in the nail holes. Wipe off almost all of the paint but leave the nail holes filled.

Music

Listen to various types of music. Is it staccato, rippling, accented—does it swell or diminish? Let your imagination catch the mood in border designs.

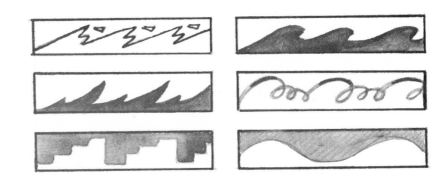

Moods In Music

Close your eyes and listen to orchestral music records. Sketch large abstract forms on newsprint that represent the music to you. Paint the mood sketches in the colors of tempera paint that the abstracts suggest. Study your choice of color and design.

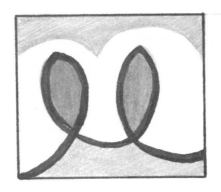

Record Album and Sheet Music Designs

Use real or imagined music titles as a base for designing record album or sheet music covers. Let the design represent the particular titles that you choose.

If possible, incorporate into your design these things: the mood of the music, a visual portrayal of the story that the music tells, and the tempo of the music.

Make your record album or sheet music cover as attractive as you can. Decorate a music room wall, a folding screen, or a bulletin board near your phonograph with these music-inspired designs.

Literature

Book Week Displays

A standing book display or book review stand is easy to make, yet is effective. A styrofoam or tagboard circle forms a base for an interlocked standard. Paper cutout story characters or the books themselves might occupy the niches.

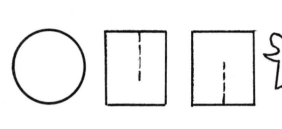

Book Covers, Bookmarks

Tie-in bookmarks may be correlated in design to handsome book covers. Sketch and color the book cover, then cut out and color a matching bookmark. Use a sturdy paper for the book cover, while white tagboard will make a good bookmark material.

Plymouth Rock

Indian Village

American History
Depicted In Shoe Box Scenes

History seems real when depicted in unusual shoe-box scenes. The top of each box is cut away to reveal miniature stage settings that portray some event in history.

Paint the bottom of the box with tempera in a scenic stage backdrop. Add pipe-cleaner figures with crepe paper clothing. Cut the top of the box as shown in an appropriate frame effect. Tape the cover to the box. Originate a number of scenes.

The Homestead

Gold-rush Days

A Fort

Health

Fruit and Vegetable Borders

Good food is important to health. Spattered drawing paper in various colors would be a lovely background for the bright fruit and vegetable cutouts. Draw fruit and vegetables on white or colored drawing papers and add details with colored pencils dipped in water. Cut these out and paste on the backgrounds. Add leaves that project beyond the edge of the background paper.

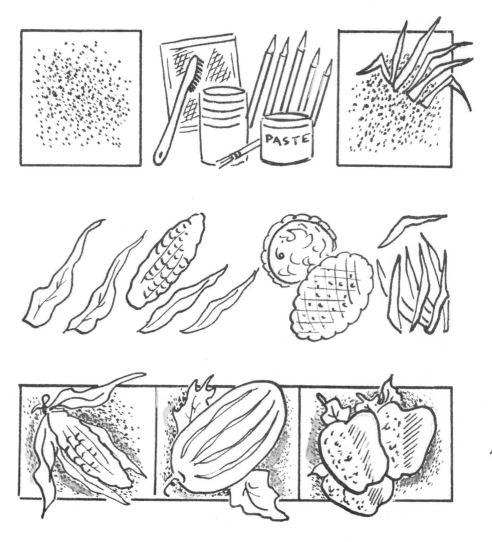

Safety

Portrayed Through The Year
With Stick Figures

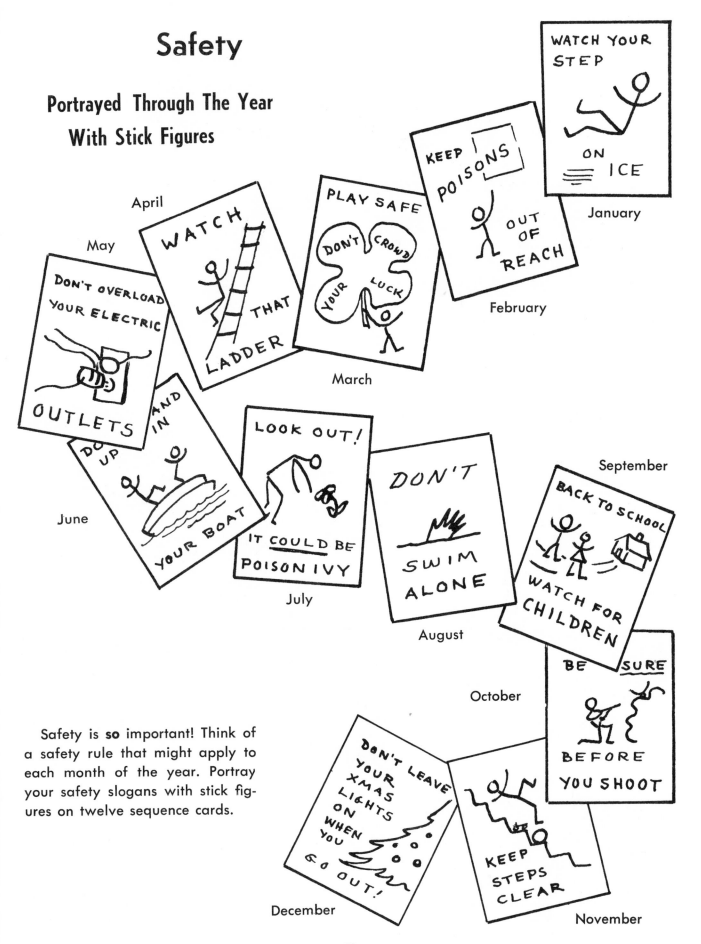

April

May

WATCH THAT LADDER

PLAY SAFE — DON'T CROWD YOUR LUCK

KEEP POISONS OUT OF REACH

WATCH YOUR STEP ON ICE

January

February

March

DON'T OVERLOAD YOUR ELECTRIC OUTLETS

DON UP AND IN YOUR BOAT

LOOK OUT! IT COULD BE POISON IVY

DON'T SWIM ALONE

BACK TO SCHOOL — WATCH FOR CHILDREN

September

June

July

August

October

BE SURE BEFORE YOU SHOOT

DON'T LEAVE YOUR XMAS LIGHTS ON WHEN YOU GO OUT!

KEEP STEPS CLEAR

December

November

Safety is **so** important! Think of a safety rule that might apply to each month of the year. Portray your safety slogans with stick figures on twelve sequence cards.

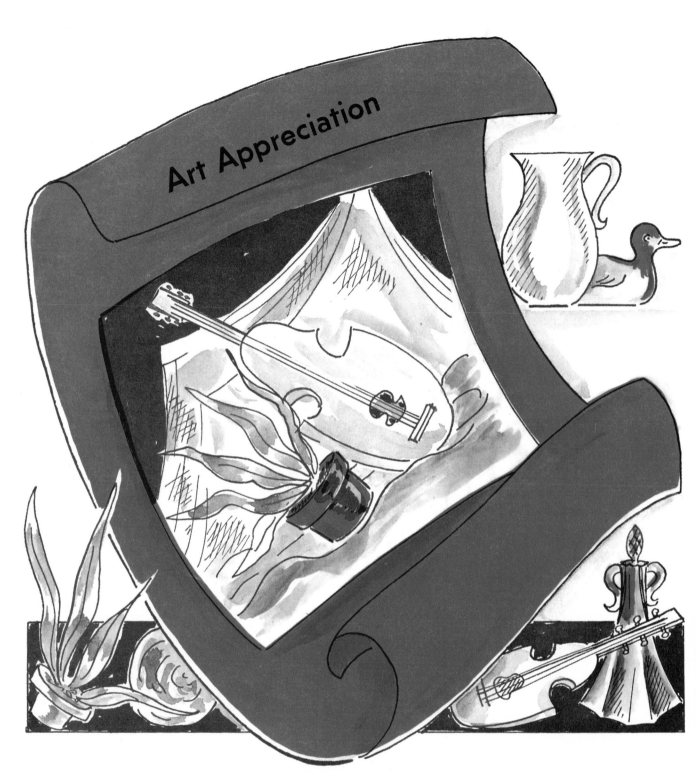

Art Appreciation

Still-life composition and practice sketching is an excellent method by which to learn art discrimination and appreciation. Select a number of vases, draperies, and interesting objects. Arrange them in still-life compositions and sketch them in a number of arrangements. Observe the effect of light and shadow, balance, perspective, color and over-all pleasure to the eye.

Section Four

Art Projects

Contents

Fall

Lovely Leaf Clusters

Indian summer can virtually move inside when leaf clusters in vivid colors and realistic squirrels are used for decoration.

Cut leaves from many colors of construction paper. Add slits as shown. Arrange in clusters by interlocking. Pin to bulletin board or tape to wall.

Door Design

Charming squirrels with bushy tails are symbolic of fall. Cut the body from deep brown construction paper. Cut the tail from light brown crepe paper and fringe the edge. Cut an acorn from a paper plate and color with crayon. Insert in the squirrel's paw.

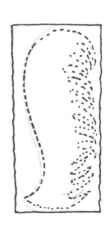

Columbus Day

A Ship In A Bottle

Shipshape—that's the word for this art project. A pale green construction paper is cut in the shape of a narrow-necked bottle. Add a blue water section on which a slit has been made as shown.

In the slit paste a red-brown ship with black masts, portholes and colorful pennants. Add heavy black thread for ship lines. Lay clear cellophane over the entire bottle to represent glass. Add deep-brown standards at the bottom.

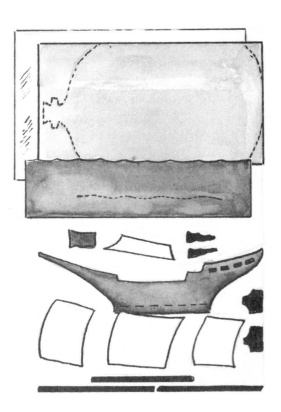

Halloween

A knotty picket fence is the meeting place of the witches' cats. On an orange background add a yellow moon. Add two long strips of brown wrapping paper for fence rails. Add crooked pickets and black cats in abundance.

The Gnarled Tree

A twisted, light-grey tree is mounted on deep-grey construction paper. Add fence and Halloween motifs.

Thanksgiving

Turkey Table Centerpiece

Paint a heavyweight paper plate with brown tempera. Flatten a yellow baking cup, cut out a wedge as shown and paste on the paper plate. Cut a turkey shape from tagboard and color with crayons. Cut an easel and glue to the back. Surround with real fruit.

Fill The Candy Jar For Christmas

With Old-fashioned Hard Candies

Remember the colorful candies of yesterday? What a variety of designs they boasted. Try your hand at designing an apothecary candy jar. Then cut circles and candy shapes and decorate with tiny designs. Paste on the jar.

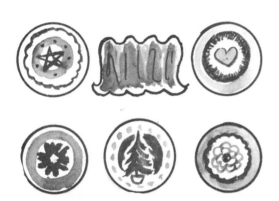

Santa In A Fringe Wreath

Cut the pieces shown in tagboard or crepe paper. Glue Santa on the crosspieces on the wreath. Fringe the crepe paper and glue to the wreath. Paste on the fringed eyebrows, hat cuff and beard.

Design Ornaments For

CHRISTMAS

Use Your Ingenuity

Draw a tall modern tree and cut from green shelf paper. Use many types of paper in assorted colors, small bells, ornaments, sequins, crepe paper, yarn, stickers, gold and silver doilies. Design an assortment of tree ornaments in as wide a variety of original types as possible.

Christmas Place Cards

Create Christmas place cards that resemble gift packages or fireplaces. Make your version of place card styles using ribbons and stickers to trim them.

New Year's Day

An Hourglass Door Decoration

Lightweight tagboard cut on the fold forms an hourglass design. Cut out the section indicated. Brush rubber cement over the lower parts of the hourglass sections. Sprinkle sugar over the cement and shake off the excess to represent sand.

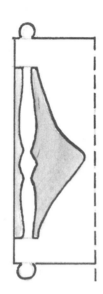

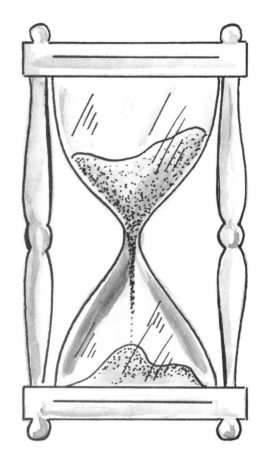

New Year's Bulletin Board

Glue silver gift paper over deep blue tagboard. Add a gold metallic ribbon bow to a gold foil paper bell. Add a Christmas ornament for a bell clanger. Draw and cut out a flesh-colored infant New Year. Paste to the background. Add the lettering with a felt tip pen.

Patriotism

A proud eagle has feather tips that project. Fold brown construction paper (9 × 12″) down the center. Sketch an eagle design, cut and open the paper flat. Use a stencil knife to make further slits as shown. Push sections out for a raised effect. Cut a laurel branch and insert in the eagle's mouth.

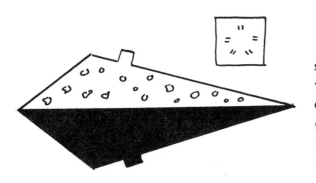

Punched Posters

Make five star points as shown from heavyweight silver foil paper. Punch one half of each point. Make slits in background paper and insert the star in a raised effect. Add gold star stickers.

Valentines

Lovebirds

These lovebirds may be used as a wall decoration, valentine or poster. Cut the bodies from white paper and mount against red construction paper. Add a silver foil, heart-shaped moon and small hearts. Run a pipe cleaner through punched holes as shown. Add crayon details.

Heart Vines

Florists' green-covered wire is used as the vine. Staple it to a white tagboard background. Add green crepe paper leaves. Cut heart flowers made from folded red paper as shown. Slip the flower tips into the slits and paste them to the background.

St. Patrick's Day

A huge, bright green shamrock sets off an Irish gentleman. Paddy has a deep-green hat, and a white pipe. His face and beard are cut as one from flesh-colored construction paper. Color the beard and hair with red crayon and fringe the edges. Add features with crayon, insert the pipe in Paddy's mouth.

March —
The Lion
Or The Lamb?

The lion or the lamb—which will bring in the month of March? Draw lion and lamb shapes and cut from construction paper. Add a fringed ruff on the lion. Add features with crayon. Cover the lamb's body with paste and sprinkle on shredded coconut for a wooly effect.

Our Parents

Mother's Silhouette

Cut a double silhouette on the fold. Design a jeweled earring using felt as a base and adding scraps of fancy braids, old jewelry, sequins, etc. Use white glue to hold in place. Print a message inside.

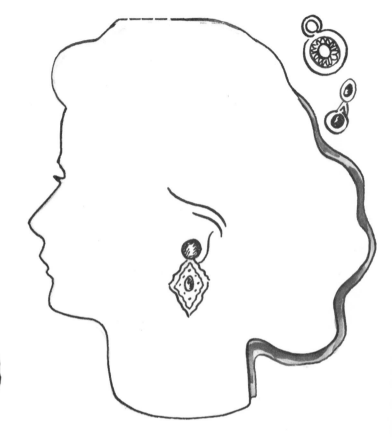

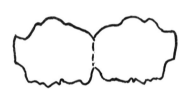

A Gift For Father

Dad would enjoy a folder as a gift—it is handy for his radio or television programs, current mail or as a place to keep his hobby clippings. Personalize the design.

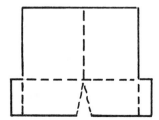 

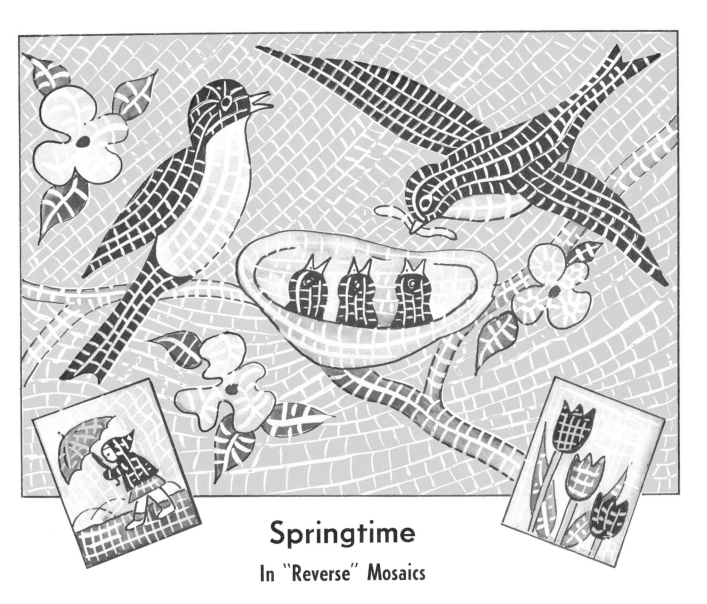

Springtime

In "Reverse" Mosaics

An unusual medium is employed here in spring posters. Draw a design on colored construction paper, add cutout motifs pasted in place. Go over the entire picture with a brush dipped in white tempera to make small lines that produce the mosaic effect.

Easter

Eggs, Eggs—Everywhere!

Try your hand at designing Easter eggs—large or small to fill many needs. Use any medium to obtain the desired effects. Display your egg designs on a simple standard—cut and slit as shown. Design some to use as Easter cards.

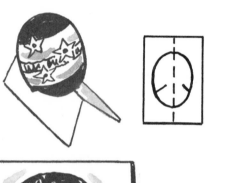

Beguiling Bunnies

This bunny-in-an-eggshell design may also be used many ways to suit your needs. Cut bunny's face, ears and paws from white construction paper. Add pink contrast inside the ears. Add the egg half, flowers, and features in any pastel Easter color. Add yarn whiskers.

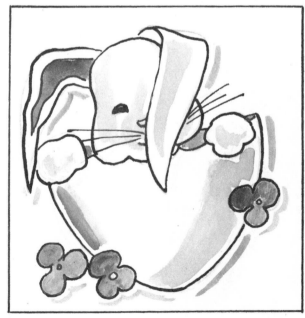

94

Dimensional Ideas

Use box halves to create unusual dimensional pictures. The ballerina is cut as shown, a crepe paper skirt is added as well as hair and stage curtains.

The race horse's head and manger are cut from tagboard. The hay is crepe paper. Postal twine is used for the halter.

The airplane in the airport scene is a section of a cardboard roll used for gift paper. The nose tip is a cone-shaped paper cup. Add paper wing and tail sections. Draw in the airport scene with crayons. Punch holes and hang with cord.

Ballerina

Airport Scene

Race Horse

Maytime

May Baskets and Maypoles

Make the May basket as shown below. Add a contrast section behind the handle. Make flowers—cutting slits on the edges. Decorate the basket. Use brads to hold the flowers in the basket and to form flower centers.

A Maypole decoration (shown above) uses two pieces of crepe paper, cut in a frame effect, as a background. Paint a yardstick to use as a Maypole. Fan ribbon streamers from the Maypole tip to the May baskets.

Stained Glass Windows

Stained glass window effects are lovely when placed where the light shines through the radiant colors. Decorate your windows for an elegant Christmas display.

Draw lines as shown in illustration A, using transparent tracing paper. Cut a frame, on the fold, from black construction paper as shown in figure B. Fold A as shown, sketch a design and repeat on the other sections. Paint the tracing paper with water colors. Use rubber cement to hold the window in the frame.

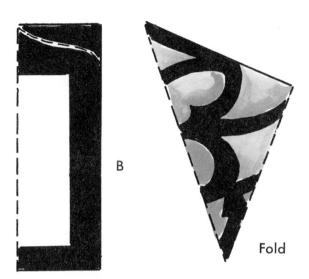

B

Fold

Completed Window

Tracing Paper

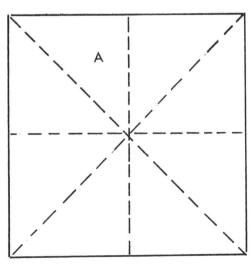

A

Action

By The Sea

Cut various shapes as illustrated and put together with brads to form sea life creatures. Make a color crayon sea scene and suspend the sea creatures on string before it.

Christmas

For Christmas make your own version of a Santa and an angel with action similar to those shown. Hang where air currents will cause them to move.

Prehistoric Animal Mobile

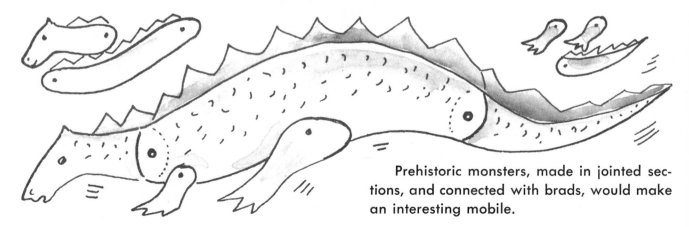

Prehistoric monsters, made in jointed sections, and connected with brads, would make an interesting mobile.

Work Portfolios

Make the folders as shown below. Decorate the fronts with tempera paint applied in wide brush strokes, that form a soft background for colorful cutout motifs. A wide, stiff brush should be used, dipped in tempera and drawn across the envelope in three strokes. Cut out construction paper motifs and paste over the tempera paint.

Brushstroke Backgrounds

Envelope

Cut this envelope 12″ × 18″ black construction paper as shown. Score the fold lines and paste the flaps in place.

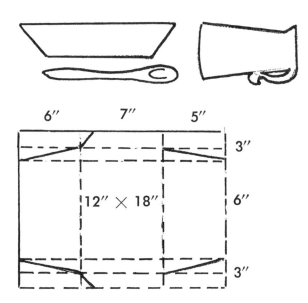

Two Pocket Folder

Use two shades of construction paper for this folder. One forms the cover, while the second (cut in two scalloped pieces as shown) becomes two pockets. Punch holes and lace with bright plastic cord.

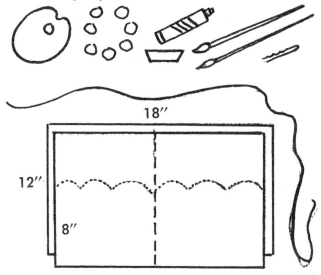

Cut-out Contrasts

Contrasting Textures

On a green tagboard background paste free-form cutouts from wallpaper, textured materials, gift papers, felt, fabric, burlap, etc. Make the largest shape first, then make each additional shape progressively smaller. See how interesting you can make your design, combining contrasting textures and colors. Some pieces might have the edges pinked or fringed with shears.

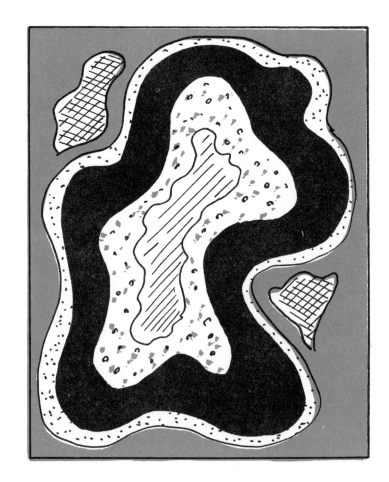

A Table Runner For Parties

Use construction paper cutout motifs, in a repeat pattern, and paste them to shiny shelf paper lengths. They are lovely to use as a table runner decoration.

Motifs may be simple or elaborate.

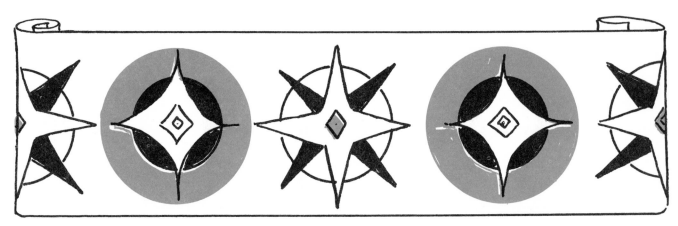

Window Decorations

Brighten your windows at any time of the year with decorative motifs. The windows shown are suggested to stimulate the creation of your own designs. Suitable materials are crepe paper, construction paper, gift tissue paper or gift wrap papers.

Floral Border

The sprightly floral border is not difficult to make. A dark green crepe paper section at the bottom has a flowerpot cutout and a scalloped top edge. Chartreuse leaves and stems are topped with multi-color tulips.

The First Snow

Deep-toned gift tissue paper has cutaway sections that allow the light to show through. Silhouette effects are successful for this medium. A snowfall scene is shown. Use rubber cement to hold the sections to the window.

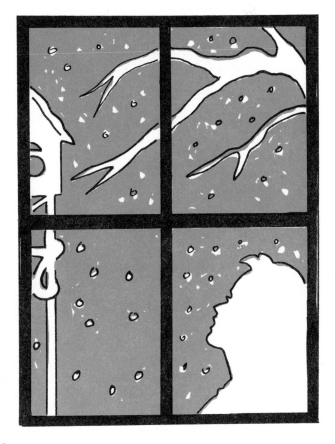

Ways To Display Art

An Easel Standard

Art "masterpieces" look well displayed on these standing-fold easels. Fold a 12″ × 18″ piece of heavy poster board as shown. Score lines before folding. Make a slit as shown and insert art work.

Shadow Frames

Effective shadow frames are easily cut from lighter weight tagboard in white or cream color. Draw lines as shown, slit as indicated and score tagboard on the fold lines. Bend in slightly to give the frame depth.

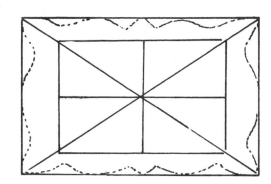

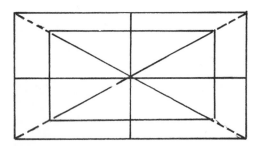

Games

A Snowball Game

Art can help entertain as illustrated by these two games. Bend a coat hanger into a circle at a right angle to the hook as shown. Decorate a large paper bag with a snow scene or snowman design. Attach the bag to the hanger with tape. Make cotton snowballs to test your guests' throwing skill.

Punched Designs

A blue-grey background is suggested. Cut a tree in two parts as shown, also an ax and cherries. Punch all pieces with a paper punch or a pointed tool for an unusual effect. Try to pin the ax (while blindfolded) in the right place.

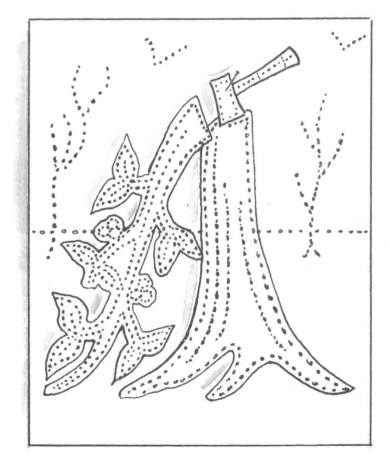

Designs From Nature

This art project employs an unusual medium. Paint heavy poster board with flat wall paint in pastel colors. Allow to dry. Choose several tones of one color and paint the board, keeping each tone in one area. While the paint is still very wet, use a blunt-tipped tool to scrape away the paint to leave the design. Work in large swirls that will carry one tone into the next area. Allow the design to dry and shellac.

Toadstools and Trees

Frost Patterns

Soaring Doves

Fish Fantasy

Triptychs

Any three-section standard may be called a triptych. The one shown above has cutout sections that produce a triple-frame effect. Glue gift wrap cellophane over the entire back. Glue designs, cut from crepe paper scraps, to the back of the clear cellophane. They will appear as paintings seen through glass.

More Triptych Ideas

Follow the small diagram to make this design. Arrange a still life or figurine display in the opening.

Scenic backgrounds are suited to this triptych. Use tracing paper with a water color scene painted on it to cover the triple openings.

Doors

Apple Sweethearts

Vary the **inside** or **outside** of your door with novel decorations. Even a closet door might serve as a background.

The apple sweethearts are cut from red construction paper—green leaves, a yellow hat, and tempera paint details set off this pair.

The name post design uses colored tape for the name post pole, florists wire for the vine, crepe paper flowers, and a white drawing paper sign.

The radiance effect converts a square door windowpane into a glamorous circular aura effect. Tagboard forms the radiance and small ornaments add a festive touch.

Masking tape in bright colors makes the tape tree.

Name Post

Radiance

Tape Tree

Parties

Invitations, Name Tags, Place Cards, Place Mats

In Free-form Design With Art Gum Motifs

Draw a design on art gum. Cut around sketch with a stencil knife. (See instructions on page 34) Press art gum on a stamp pad and imprint the design on free-form party accessories as shown. Construction paper might be used for this project.

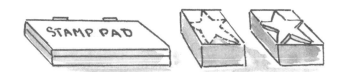

Place Cards and Matching Place Mats

These place mats may be made of shelf paper. The place cards are tagboard. Unify the design of both pieces. Vary the motif to suit the occasion.

Party Decorations

A cheesecloth or fish net swag is a perennial party accessory. Christmas ornaments, tagboard sea creatures, crepe paper butterflies—or countless other variations might be hung on this drape background.

Variations

Paper Link Designs

Almost any motif would be enhanced by an edging of paper chain links. Mexican sombreros, such as illustrated, are made of tagboard and have small slits all along the edge with paper links slipped through and then pasted to make a fringe effect. A crepe paper serape could also have a paper link fringe. O—La!

Bulletin Boards

Unusual bulletin board treatments stimulate interest in activities. The reindeer scene has a shiny green shelfpaper evergreen pasted over a construction paper background in blue and white. A brown deer surveys tiny cotton tufts that are pasted over the entire scene.

The tepee of brown wrapping paper serves as a news exchange medium. Use chalk to add the campfire and tent decorations.

The carnival clown is pasted in a real carton that is stapled to the bulletin board. A scalloped background sets off his bright colors. He holds a pleated paper accordion and has a neck ruff of crepe paper.

Reindeer

Tepee

Jack-In-The-Box

INDEX

INDEX Continued